Chittagong

Chittagong

Poems
and Essays

Cameron Conaway

Iris Press
Oak Ridge, Tennessee

Cover Photograph by Pierre Torset
For more information visit: pierretorset.com

Book Design by Robert B. Cumming, Jr.

Library of Congress Cataloging-in-Publication Data

Conaway, Cameron.
    [Poems. Selections]
    Chittagong : poems / Cameron Conaway.
        pages ; cm
    ISBN 978-1-60454-225-7 (pbk. : alk. paper)
    I. Title.
    PS3603.O53215A6 2014
    811'.6—dc23
                        2014035099

For Chittagong

Contents

"…our minds have instructed our eyes to see."

—Muhammad Yunus
Chittagonian, pioneer of microcredit,
awarded the 2006 Nobel Peace Prize

Looking for Allah

I'm an hour outside of Chittagong, Bangladesh. That's a guess. The bus broke down in a tiny little town with a whole lot of people. More people than blades of grass. More people than all the molecules of scent that swirl around me: exhaust, ripe mango, salted lassi, rotten mango, curry, worry. I'm here for a story.

I mean *right now* I'm surrounded by cows and sitting next to this dude who is selling lychees because, as it turns out, buses are like us humans—when they're asked to do too much and not shown love they break down.

I lied earlier...

...about there being more grass blades than people. Because I'm so new it seems to me that the people here have the capacity to be three. This dude beside me selling lychees *is* the dude beside me selling lychees but he also appears to be his blazing white footlong beard and his deshi mahoba red mouth which, when it catches flecks of sunlight, burns with a kind of unfamiliar brightness that makes me look at it as though it's entirely separate from him.

I am trying to get to Chittagong to see and write about the infamous shipbreaking yards. As it turns out, the world's largest ships are also like us—they have birthdays. They are developed over the course of many months, given a name and when they are ready they are nudged out into the ocean with a bottle of champagne. It's happy birthday, and the clock of age starts ticking. Because like or unlike us, most of these ships have predestined dates of death. When they turn 29-years-old it's time. Their life of holding oil or champagne-drinking vacationers comes to an end. There's a good chance their next stop will be Chittagong (Bangladesh's busiest seaport), one home of many along the world's largest bay, the Bay of Bengal.

Hundreds of barely-paid boys and men will gather their hammers and blowtorches to break the beast down piece-by-piece, draining the asbestos and the oil and a host of toxic unpronunciations straight into the sand and ocean. After about six months of metal-to-metal music, 24-hour-a-day human labor, the ship that once looked like a hotel horizontal will exist only as its million little pieces. It'll be spread all over the country and all over the world. The blade that swirls in your smoothie blender.

I look up at my lychee friend, ask, "Chittagong?" and he points to the green tuk-tuk, called a CNG, that sits lonely on the other side of the dusty road. I walk over and the driver is sleeping; I stand there not knowing what to do. Then out of the blue my lychee friend appears beside me. He wakes up the driver by putting a huge jackfruit on his lap. They both laugh, and I hear them say "Chittagong" multiples times. With that, the driver motions for me to get in, and my lychee friend flashes the most beautiful red smile I've ever seen. The engine sputters, kicks, turns over and we're off, leaving a trail of dust behind us and hopefully getting closer to where I want to go.

"Where you from?" the driver asks in unexpectedly good English.

After a startled pause, "U.S.A." I say.

"Obama!" he says with, you guessed it, a red mouth.

"Obama!" I say, laughing and leaning into this human connection.

"Are you a follower of Jesus?" he asks.

"No, I wouldn't say that."

"Well then are you a follower of Buddha?"

"No, I wouldn't say that either."

"Then surely you are a follower of Allah?"

"Nope. I am not a follower of Jesus, Buddha or Allah."

"If you don't have Jesus, Buddha or Allah then you have nothing. How worthless are you?" He somehow says this while still maintaining his inquisitive tone.

I say nothing, uncomfortably start leafing through the blank pages of my notebook.

"Wow! So you don't have Jesus, Buddha or Allah," he says more to himself than to me.

More silence. I think of so many things to say that I say nothing. At this point we're cruising on the open road and the engine is so loud that if we want to be heard it'll take a yell.

"Are you at least looking for Allah?" he yells over the engine. The veins in his neck bulge and I hope it's from his need to be loud.

I mumble "Jesus Christ-O-Mighty" under my breath, already tired of where this conversation is going.

"Where do I look?" I ask.

"Allah is everywhere," he says. "If you are looking for Allah you will find Allah."

My hope about his veins didn't pan out. His tone is becoming more hostile with each kilometer we cover.

"Well what do you do? What brings you to our land of Allah?"

"I am a poet," I say. "I am here to write poetry."

"Poet." He says this to himself as though trying to figure out what it means in English. And then he yells, "Kobi! Kobi!"

"You write poems?" he asks. He takes his hands off the wheel to act like he's writing something.

"Yes, yes, I write poems," I say. Total tone change. The choppy waters are no more.

"Wow! A poet! A real poet!" He flashes a red smile that I must admit, in this moment, puts to shame the smile of my lychee friend.

"You do not need to go looking for Allah," he says. "Jesus was a poet, Buddha was a poet, Allah was a poet. If you are a poet then you do not need to go looking for them because they are already inside of you. Welcome to Bangladesh. We are happy to have you here!"

And this is when we both lose it. We're laughing so hard that his face is nearly pressed against the steering wheel and my abdominal muscles are on fire.

Another CNG pulls up beside us and my driver points toward me in the back, yells, "Kobi! Kobi!" and the other driver flashes a red smile and gives me a thumbs up before he speeds on ahead of us. A few kilometers later a sign appears, one of many, one that I am not still trying to unpack years later: Welcome to Chittagong.

Maybe Man

—*For Mahabubur, Abdul Malek Road corner, Chittagong*

His beard an inch of white
at root and eight more yellow.

A light lychee bushel hanging
from rusted nail rolls to fall.

He tilts his head and presses on
his inner brow with his thumb

and I sense his stress entirely
wrong. His thumb slides across

to wring his brow like a rag.
No drips, a splash, two fists

gather to retie his lungi.
He looks at me like yesterday

when I said "maybe tomorrow"
but meant "not now, I'm tired."

Today, even his eyes have ribs
so when they looked at me

and he said "maybe tomorrow?"
but meant "please, please buy"

I sat beside him at his stall,
emptied my wallet of taka

and we peeled back the rough
lychee skin to sweet bursting.

Telling Time

A mosquito floats
dead in the white
rice bowl in the sink.
Outside, sirens sing
songs of the broken
and streetlights spark
off and buzz on until
hammer and birdsong.

GROWL

I saw the bang of the broken
black irises so black they masked
the pupils that by morning or mid-day
blazed the sclera yellow of teeth
and truth from the music of exhaust
and the lost garbage trucks
and the watercolor wild streets airs
and the rusted browns and the rust itself
and the old and crusted black cats
and the beautiful people people people
who had nothing but nothing for
and until so goddamn long.

Saw evaporation rise from the quadriceps
of a rickshaw puller and smell
of curry and lend moisture and flavor
to the dusty dirt road drama
in exchange for its unfolding before us.

Saw the whole world of a place be used
but take the shape of diamonds through
the duct-taped cages of its green CNG's.

I heard toxic paint sing the song of wildlife
and the ocean roll with the breath of death.

Took cha and biscuit with boys triple
their own age and with too poors
and alone in the dirt and with the dragging
white beards of elders bent to all fours
and cha and biscuit on corrugated iron roofs
and in rotted bamboo huts with newborns
and with tiny children whose trapezius
muscles burst to their ears from hard labor

and with dying wizards so red in tooth
and mouth from deshi mahoba and the toll
of toiling that they looked like they'd taken
a bite from the fresh neck veins of the cow
along the trail after the dog had finished
humping the bloody tangle of it all
while barking to the dogs watching
or waiting to keep their space right now
because this *this* was his now in the then
Japanese Air Force bombs boom in April
and December and then in now the Famine
of 43' felt before me as I carried computer
and camera and cell phone and mosquito spray
and wad of taka and my dripping privileges
to fishing villages stocked only with dried
and drying water and wood and humans.

Saw the handicapped wander the hill tracts
forever scarred by cerebral malaria or the blind
luck of being born here at this time and with
this set of twisted genetics and told to deal.

Saw a blind man record audiobooks and see
the joy of contributing something to someone
and express the joy from kicking my ass
in a typing competition while the sweet scent
of deep-fried and sugared balls of dough
wafted from the village down the road
courtesy of the chef
his blind and deaf twin brother.

Saw an eighty-year-old stroke patient walk
again after three months of crawling on floors
and two more in rehab
saw her eyes fill with tears at each sliding step
at my awe at each of her sliding steps

and if there is a god may it let her die
while standing because she will find joy
in dying with triumph trickling in her bones
as she leans against a wall with legs locked
and smiles into something or nowhere else.

Found a café with WiFi one day
logged into Facebook
saw my grandmother liked my status.
Found a café with WiFi another day
logged into Facebook
saw my grandmother had died.

Saw signs and followed them and they took me
to places that once were but were no longer
or to places that simply never were like the hotel
and restaurant that never once cooked food
or that at no point had any available rooms.

Saw all of July in the empty coconut shell
the kids stripped from the mouth of a goat
so they could play a pick-up game of cricket
where the bowler and wicket-keeper spots
were marked by trash so pungent it stung
the eyes and gave rise to spontaneous maggots
and stories that will gather like hair in drains
before sleeping in the black crow's caw.

Been granted access into no access and no access
into excess and it was here where street cripples
nudged me with their stumps for ten taka or spoke
specks of their rotted gums into the corners
of my eyes as they helped me find the right bus.

Felt worthless by having and wanting
to give in a way that didn't merely prolong
this right here but I could not make fishing nets

or offer better employment to the sewers
enslaved in factories by the brands so dear to us
that they are intertwined into the fabrics
of our lives.

Saw those nearing the end stand for me
the *kobi*
Bangla for poet
because they respect the art though illiterate
stood for me by the hundreds as I made my way
with sweaty notebook to each of them
filled with questions and dizzy with thirst
and wanting to but making no promises
because the pressure in this heat
and reflecting in their sweatbeads
would have killed the moment and the parts
of us that are inside each other.

The toxic paint sung the song of silence
and the ocean spumed with black bubbles.

Felt weak as osteoporotic women
in full Muslim dress
carried stacks of concrete bags
atop their heads and never once
like me
let out sighs from the heat or the hardness
or of life's circumstance or of needing
a want so the nonstop clanks and drills
and floating debris of construction
every somewhere would curl
into
settle.

Saw a corpse bake in the heat until skin
at clavicle gave and let bone's bright white
out from its wrapping and then the ants

the black ants danced from blackened
to shadow until shadowmelt kissed asphalt.

Saw the dog whose eyes were still curious
and whose face held the spirit of the growl
though its pink roll of organ lay neatly coiled
a foot from where they once were held
and how they now held the tire's imprints.

The growl of the broken in the eyes still open.

Never sensed a *not again* when the communal rice
bowl was set in table's middle and we strangers
dug in with right hands only and shoveled
finger scoops into our mouth at orange
mornings and if we were lucky once more
when liquid night filled the space between us all
with black and buzz and a crunch to the white
that wasn't there in morning but those bodies
made it easier to get through the netted nights
where the dreams of hands moved through me
like the warmth of grandma's that hugged
the freezepop after she handed it to me.

Saw countless women who said their name
was Bibi Ayesha and I heard their stories
and though some were different their lines
all shaped by the same sun and the same work
were all the same at the eyes and the nose
and the back of the neck and it is these people
all of them
and this place
all of it
that inspired
because something about being famously
inspiring dulls it all
something about anonymity in the hills or huts

grinding days down to rice
without caring who is watching
squatting to masturbate out in the open
into the city drainage ditches that roll with froth
and rat hair and cum and shit and the blood
of slaughtered animals
something about the deep squatting
out in the fields alongside your brothers to all
shit together because for centuries you have
all worked and taken rice at the same times
and endured each other's struggles and carried on
each other's flesh each other's clockworked lives.

The song of silence was a whisper's urn
and the ocean's churn burned to quiver.

Something about all the *dis*
the displaced from 91' cyclone or yesterday's floods
the disabled and the disenchanted who have seen
the glimpses of otherness
on the magazine covers they use to divert the rains.

Something about the beautiful woman in her prime
who vomited violently and heavied a plastic bag
beside me for the duration of a five-hour bus ride
to Cox's Bazar yet never once showed the strife
on her face that peeled across mine for her.

Something about the scent of that vomit
of blued bread
of curried and mold furry orange peels
of fennel seed and fish
of meat after heat flies
and how it all didn't so much gag me as fit.

Something about how the NGOs offer loans for cows
and lend to those who never have so the poor reach

an even lower level of enslavement
something about the other
NGOs that fight for the trafficked boy who was
blindfolded for three days and beaten
or the mentally disabled teenage girl who was sold
to a mobile brothel or the area of ocean blackened
by toxic unpronunciations.

Something about how the work turns clothing
to the same color as the worker's skin
how logos carry the stripes of the Bengal tiger
how the rawness is the soundtrack as hut schoolkids
sing *we shall overcome*
we shall overcome
we shall overcome
over and over while cows moo
and the smell of shit in barn and pants at once moves
as notes through thick alfalfa air and drags as the legless
reflect in their eyes while soundspace is filled with the hawks
of men clearing the endless phlegm from their throats
and swishing it around to clear the tartar and then
spitting it on the roads or at market or from atop
the bamboo bone scaffolding of a coming soon resort.

No song but the storm.
No ocean but the mud.

Saw the old dig beside damn-near babies in trash heaps
both looking for want though want couldn't be found there.

Saw the crazy get beat with scrap metal but mostly provide
laughter even while people starve or disease dwindle down
or are losing their own minds.

Saw newspapers declare the need for plans sustainable
ten years worth
while outside most barely sustain until sundown.

Had villagers beg me for legal documents to claim
stability in the most unstable lands in the world.

Saw an activist pen a document about anti child labor
while a child served him food and wiped the table.

Saw sweat drip like light rain as workers on bamboo
ladders pounded away and how I felt as my own
sweat smelled of the same curry as those
upperclass who can afford meat and spice.

Something about how humming comes from all corners
folksongs memorized by people
to sear on and awash the madness with beat.

Something about the beat.

How fathers leave as my own but leave for dead
to Dhaka or to a falsely promised job which now
has them eating bread crumbs from Pakistani jail
floors or leave because they had too many
kids and are embarrassed at their inability to provide
or leave because memory pain dusts
easier than place pain in your face.

Saw mothers cleave no matter what even when their hip
bones bulged with some cancer or growths protruded
from their necks
how mothers do not leave
until they die and even then they are like the crow
that sits atop the bull's backbone.

How the mothers do not leave
even towels hang on the line too long.

Saw acting troupes roll through to show family
planning or bring laughter to the woman who fifteen

minutes prior got a finger prick for her fever
and now knows she has the deadliest form of malaria.

How flies land on you with wet legs from the sweat
of someone else's forearm.

How the tear of naan feels like lust in love
and how after meals toothpicks fill the space
between bowls and plates and how there is not
an abundance of anything but these toothpicks
and how ninety are offered but one is needed
and how the dogs know dinner is finished
when the toothpicks sing and how they circle
as clouds gather and how the drainage ditches
follow you like guilt and wrap their scabs and clog
and necessity and how what the shoulder knows
is all we really need to know
distributing weight rather than taking it all
giving when needed and staying sturdy when needed
and how gangrene creeps into even the wisest
and how workers in the back of dump trucks
dig deep to fill sand bags at forty miles per hour.

How one hut mother taught writing with twigs
fill in the gap she'd say *fill in the gap* and she would break
sticks to form a letter and four more to fill the square
and the children worked hard to fill the gaps with letters
and the gaps my goodness the gaps and the lean rats
took my shoes while the gecko chirp steadied
my breath and the whitest lamb wrestled
with the mangiest black puppy and how men rolled
up their lungis and entered flood waters to push
the CNG out and how their toenails leaked pus
and how naked children too large to be naked
ran around the construction site of a hotel
that will house the world's wealthiest monied

and how the long breathless breathless breathless
mosque prayers played to the beat of the sewing
machine and a hut's many colors of shyness
and the stirring of a mill and the crickets
and cricket players and of construction and crows
and horns horns horns and the hawks and the hawking
hawked phlegm ever-rolling like the rickshaw and the signs:

Chittagong: The Shiny New Destination
For Your Outsourcing.

No song but the grating.
No ocean but the weight.

The seeds of growl in the wince.

A country proud of Liberation 71'
begging for slave labor and fighting against it.

No shine because shine is an individual thing
and there is no individual thing here only the beauty
of everything colliding and blending
the whirling and whirring dust of togetherness
the knowledge
that civilization is but a way to hide the shit and penis
the breast and the beast of reality
a mask so we can get behind our vulnerabilities
to blind one type of beautiful and bloom another.

Fast Twitch Grief

Grief is brief
repeatedly. Open the window
for fresh air and there—
peripherals catch sliver of sunflower
and that's it. Gram's backyard.
Sunflower lit by the sun, her care.
Ripe pears on the kitchen table.
The underwear I accidentally
sharted in and tried to sneakily
clean in the sink. Pap squeaking
away in his recliner and the Avon
forms on the floor by the front door.
And there's a knock.
And I'm back in Chittagong.
And the hotel manager gives me
a fresh mango smoothie so bright
it's as though it swallowed the light.

Fast Twitch Travel

You are in Kyoto (or Altoona) and you see a kimono (or robe) and you feel its fabric in your hands, make your way to price tag. You can't afford it. Made in Japan (or Pennsylvania). But the one beside it is fewer of thread.

Will do just fine. You can afford it. Made in Bangladesh. And that's it. You're back to collapsed factory. Bodies in rubble. Jackson Pollock's Naked Man with Knife. The tired *how they need those jobs to survive* argument. You're back to torn—that river of mind where your toes don't touch. And there's a "Can I help you with anything?" and you're back to now. The store employee offering you a trying so bright it's as though they swallowed the light.

What the River Takes

For Mitu and the late Naddu
Jamuna River, Bangladesh

They are called char
and they take char—

a gristled and ligamented
patience that takes

and pulls back the scapula
of the children it layers

too young with muscle.
It is the cycle of life

taken to total breaking
speeds, land to plant

life one day and the next
a wave of salted silt ripe

only with hunger.

With each drag it takes
itself into itself and leaves

a crested smile of land—
forgiveness for the soil

it gave and took not
of promises or promise

in blood of parent to baby—
not knowing there is *no*

and there is no taking
back from where our tides

rolled in for we do not go
gentle into any kind of night.

PAUSING SHARON OLDS

There, when the touching of your lips
is the size of the cursor. Pause.
That's the space where no words
can be made but the guttural,
which I knew wouldn't happen,
of course, because I knew the future
and still craved it, knew the next
line and knew even knowings are always
new due to life and time, and rewind.
I gleaked on you after that first taste
of jackfruit in the morning, ran my
warm finger over the nape of your neck
to clean the screen, left you to let
the dog out to piss, pop the bread
in the toaster and make a peanut
butter and jelly sandwich and you,
Sharon, stayed perfectly patiently still,
my own pixelated portable poetry doll.
Now I've paused you to do other things,
say, less sanitary than licking
this morning's PB knife clean before
plunging it into the jelly jar, but we
have many memories together separately,
like the time you spoke of douchebags
as the fevered woman beside me on the bus
in Chittagong vomited her curry and lassi
into a plastic bag from Khulshi Mart.
Or the time I meant to drag all three
inches of you across the screen
but accidentally clicked an advertisement
for flavored condoms. Then the time
when, as the galaxy you were transposed
onto buffered, I imagined you inside a shot
glass, reaching up high to the lip to pull

yourself out and then tipping over
the whole damn thing. Rest assured,
Sharon, my playing you never made
Stag's Leap fade, never made *Strike
Sparks* moist. Unpause. The line break
this morning was 9-minutes but this
morning is, like, so yesterday. Moments
ago I sat front row, saw you read, for real.
I couldn't move because you were moving
me, dragging me across the deep ecology
of your loss then into the public bedroom
of private humor. This is our relationship:
You, tube, standing in squares, reading
into microphones the size of pen tips.
Me, maximizing your dimensions, pausing
you, which is the worst part, pausing you,
which is the best part, pausing to absorb
you as the world warms, putting you to sleep
while charging you so you may charge me.

Of Ships and Men

There are ships like hotels horizontal
and there are children and children

breaking, dragging these dead vessels
through beach sand soiled with oil

through the swirling peace rainbows
of slavery, a six month deconstruction

of scrap metal and tiny little lives
scraping by one then two then twenty

broken walls of asbestos at a time
when there is no gear, no gloves

and masks only of signage bold fronted
"No Child Labour, We Take Safety First"

while Nasima, 8, of Chandan Baisha,
tries to hide just beyond the gates.

Bits of rust from the iron plates jump
into my eyes. Tomorrow? Don't know.

We have too much work to do today.
And Sohel, 11, who came from Comilla:

My mother works at the jute mill and I
started working last year at the yards

as a cutter helper. My father never visits.
He sometimes looks for me in the streets

and tries talking to me, but I refuse.
He harmed my mother too much.

In the village, no work. Here, work.
My ambition is high. I want to become

a cutter-helper. Maybe in five years.
And Robani, 1 2, from Moheshkali Island

who left his village to come here after
the river took his family's strip of land,

who watched as his father was crushed
by some falling part from the floating

dustbin, who saw his father's shinbone
jutting white out from temple red

and who was told by the foreman
Your father was too weak for this job.

Now is your time to be the real man
of your family, a strong man that does

not break. Robani recalls not the years
when he and his father caught fish

or the time they played hours of cricket
with a bamboo bat and old compass case

but of that white and red mangle of man.
At night as he sleeps he hears orders

and he hears the hushed sound of heavy
steel ship part thump into black sand,

the sound that killed his father as if
his father had not stood between

the black steel and the blacker sand,
the weight of it all so fast that a man

can't sound, no moan, no emotion,
bones and memories and history ground,

crumpled quietly, unlike a paper sheet
loud in crumpling and capable of reuse

or the *sagor* waves out beyond the black
or the thunder or of an echo which is

not even alive but an imitation, nope,
his father was pestled silently unlike

the rice or flour or tea or other fined
things at the mad market. How much

to buy the silence of a man crippled?
Depends on how crippled. 10,000 taka

if one can still walk, talk, use both arms.
It's been forty years since the first vessel.

No facts for flesh, only for things metaled:

Bangladesh is world's largest shipbreaker.
Bangladesh is world's first shipbreaker.

Gets 30% of steel shipbreaking.
Has thousands of jobs from shipbreaking.

But what of shipbreaking beating out
child prostitution in dangerous jobs?

Or the people, miles away from the yards,
who have for generations survived on

fish that are no longer? Their choice:
be broken by labor or by starvation.

What of how 20% of the workers
are preadolescent boys? Or the activist

who knows Chittagong needs these ships
but wants only safety and no child labor,

who says to me: *You watch. When they
kill me nobody will care. One replaces*

*another here. The steel of these beasts
has shaped more than our men's bodies.*

Of Ships and Men: An Essay

"The supervisor beats us."
"I have swallowed much fume. When you have gas inside your body you can't eat."
"I drink water, but it's so polluted I feel that I drink metal. I have no choice."
"When I'm lying on my bed the images of the dead come back."

Emaciated men with torn clothing, dulled eyes and missing fingers carry cables caked with rust on bare shoulders made browner with dried blood. Scarred young boys in toxic slick mud up to their knees drag themselves barefoot into the oiled earth to find sharp scraps of iron. The June heat blazes here and seems to thicken the polluted air and louden the blasting and pounding. Atop ships far larger than I ever imagined are men the size of fingernails. Security guards dressed in blue leaf camouflage and strapped with semi-automatic machine guns stand at the gates in front of weathered billboards that read: "No Child Labour, We Take Safety First."

Viscerally, it's all too clear. Slavery exists here. As does exploitative child labor. And black ocean waters. And black plume skies brightened only with blowtorch flame. The industry seems to flaunt its illegalities like badges of honor. I'm not the first to paint the hell-on-earth picture of "the yards" and hopefully I'm not the last. But while pictures may be worth a thousand words they can't share a full-bodied story the way Daniel Schorn of *CBS* did in 2009. His opening paragraph has become the mantra of those looking to reform the shipbreaking industry:

"We all know how ships are born, how majestic vessels are nudged into the ocean with a bottle of champagne. But few of us know how they die. And hundreds of ships meet their death every year. From five-star ocean liners, to grubby freighters, literally dumped with all their steel, their asbestos, their toxins on the beaches of some of the poorest countries in the world, countries like Bangladesh."

Though I came to Chittagong to study Bangladesh's efforts to combat malaria among the hill tract people for a book I'm writing titled *Malaria: Poems*, I quickly became enthralled with shipbreaking. I'd never heard of it or even thought about what happens to old ships until I began researching

Chittagong, and even then I naively assumed that because the *BBC* and others had internationally lambasted it that, ya know, things had been fixed.

My first impression of the yards was one of fear. The ships are the size of buildings and tilted at all sorts of angles due to the wet sand. It seemed that they had to fall, that no matter how they fell they could crush people within miles on all sides. Once the fear receded disappointment rushed in. First it was an unfounded disappointment at the local community for sitting back and allowing this to continue. Second was disappointment in the international community for not stepping in with the mighty world-policing powers of which I'm rarely a fan. Third was disappointment at the craft to which I've given a considerable portion of my life. *Terrific writers have covered this problem,* I thought to myself as I gazed out into the madness, *yet it is still here menacing in my face and ugly as hell.* This last disappointment of course became a personal disappointment. *What the hell am I doing with my life?*

Muhammad Ali Shahin is the Program Manager for Advocacy at Young Power in Social Action (YPSA) in Chittagong. YPSA is by far the most diverse and effective NGO I've come across in all my travels. Through them I saw stroke patients they had rehabilitated cry with joy at each step because of their ability to walk again. I met tribespeople in secluded mountains who no longer feared malaria because YPSA had provided them with nets and a clinic at the bottom of the hill. I met an entire community of blind people thrilled to have a purpose in life now that YPSA had trained them how to type and create audiobooks from textbooks—they were working to create audio lectures on family planning when I first met them. Though YPSA has programs in HIV/AIDS prevention, sustainable economic development, anti-malaria efforts and support for disabled peoples, among others, Muhammad specializes in the shipbreaking industry and it was clear why within two minutes of meeting him.

"I know you have questions but let me first give you these pictures," he said as he handed me a stack of about twenty framed photographs. He sat down beside me, put a humongous fan on the chair in front of us and turned it on full blast. "You ready?" he asked, his voice undulating through the fan's blades. I nodded yes and so it began.

Each picture contained stories within stories. On a black-and-white picture of a man in a hospital room: "I was there the day it happened. A ship part fell and nearly split his head in half. I saw bits of his brain. We rushed him to the hospital and told his family and they were all scared to death that they'd have to sell their land and cows and house for treatment that may not work. I went to the shipbreaking boss and totally lost it. 'Your worker is dying from that damn yard and through no fault of his own. Get in here and cover these costs or else you will find yourself in every single newspaper in the world by tomorrow morning!'"

And on he went. One incredible story after another. Muhammad was no reciting robot either, he told all of these as though for the first time and with most stories I saw tears filling his eyes. It made me wonder if the fan was to cool us off or to dry tears. I admit using it for both.

"At 29 years-of-age most ships by law must be broken down and Chittagong is considered the #1 place in the world where this happens," he said.

"Where do the workers come from?"

"They are migrant men and boys coming from some of the poorest regions in Bangladesh. They are considered machines; if one dies another will replace him. They live up to twenty in small huts often lacking sanitation. They are contract workers and are in no way given the opportunity to organize themselves; trade unions are not allowed. There is no complete recording of accidents or death at the shipbreaking yards; dead and non-identified workers still get thrown out to sea, leaving a widow and children with no news and no income."

Silence was the only language we could speak after such a statement. I pressed on in a slightly different direction: "I know Syeda Rizwana Hasan won the 2009 Goldman Prize, which is basically the Nobel Prize for Environment. Because of this, aren't there laws the shipbreaking owners have to abide by in terms of environmental impact?"

"Oh yes. There are a bunch of laws that either aren't maintained or are filled with loopholes. Some laws state that ships have to be pre-cleaned of any toxic substances before being sent here. Doesn't happen. According to the Environment Conservation Act, an industry like shipbreaking is supposed to take certain environmental measures to break a ship, but they don't. And because its standards are not maintained in the yards, provisions in the Labour Act have also been categorically violated.

It must further be understood that the shipbreaking industry, as many other areas of Bangladeshi reality, is corrupt. Mafia-like structures are controlling the yards and in collusion with some government officials they are earning enormous sums of money. As an informal sector shipbreaking avoids having to comply with existing labor legislation; as an informal sector shipbreakers also have to pay high taxes. It seems therefore that the yard owners pay for a blind governmental eye. The ship-owners are making huge profits as well by selling their ships to Bangladesh. These profits too are corrupt as many ship-owners hide behind post-box companies registered in countries that turn a blind eye to existing human rights and environmental legislation."

"What are the actual environmental impacts? Have you had researchers come in?" I asked. "I saw what I saw and it was gross but it seems the guards with machine guns..." I trailed off.

"Everyone in the world relies on the ocean whether they realize it or not. Nowhere is this clearer than Chittagong. Most of the materials on ships such as asbestos, PCBs, lead, cadmium, organotins, arsenic, zinc and chromium, black oil and burned oil have been defined as hazardous waste under the Basel Convention. Many of our people survive solely on fish that now no longer exist because these ships are being cut up by hand and on open beaches and with no consideration given to safe and environmentally-friendly waste management practices. Something like this ensures that a developing country stays forever developing...."

"It seems that the developed countries, in one sense, are creating employment here in a way that provides a short-term paycheck yet long-term and irreversible consequences. What can be done of this?"

"The polluter pays principle must be enforced. It must be. Developed countries should take responsibility for pre-cleaning vessels as far as possible before exporting them to developing countries. Poor countries and their territories are not dustbins or a dumping place for the developed world. This only widens the gap between rich and poor. People who live in developing countries have the same right to a decent job and they too need to breathe fresh air. Believe me when I say that Bangladesh has enough problems to deal with. We are one of the countries suffering the most from climate change resulting from the developed world's CO_2

emissions, not our emissions. Waste emission from shipbreaking is not our waste."

"What would you say to someone who says you simply want to end this industry completely?"

"NGOs and media have been campaigning for so many years on this shipbreaking issue and they've never urged an end to the industry. They simply urged for national and international labor and environmental laws to be respected and enforced. If somebody is saying that NGOs want to stop shipbreaking then we have to assume that the yard owners and international players of shipbreaking want to avoid the compliance issues by blaming NGOs.

The highest court of Bangladesh also gave orders in line with the Basel Convention but there have been little if any changes to the hazardous practices. Yes, this industry provides much of our resource needs. Yes, it employs a ton of our people. But all of this should not come with a stipulation that says our ocean will be destroyed and our men and boys will be subject to hell-on-earth. Do I want the industry to end? Of course not. But if it won't follow some very basic rules regarding human rights then it shouldn't exist whatsoever. We are poor but first we are humans."

What I saw remains burned in my brain even a full month later. When I see dilapidated houses I see ships. When I saw a rainbow last week I saw the rainbow swirls of oil on top of the ocean. Although I know that the ocean, decimated by this process, will spread these men's struggle to everyone in the country, it is the children working on the yards that still rip at my emotions. Their faces. Their little scarred bodies. The billboards in English that stood on the legs of mockery: "No Child Labour."

***

Opening Quotes: International Federation for Human Rights, Childbreaking Yards: Child Labour in the Ship Recycling Industry in Bangladesh, 2011

Original Publication Date: July 19, 2012

Things Break Apart

Death for dancing?

The morning's thought occurred before the electricity blew and that powering down sound reached my heart's valves. The loose, lopsided wall fan wobbled its dust-crusted self to an uneven stop. Gecko chirp startled but this was only because the soft pulsing hum of the old air conditioner, now off, served both as great cooler and great muffler. Rest was granted to the small television whose fuzzy feed seemed to put all characters underwater, including the news reporters in its finale who spoke not of events here in Chittagong but of those in the mountainous district of Kohistan in northern Pakistan, where a traditional jirga, or tribal council, had sentenced six people to death because the rhythm of moment entered their porous bones and they gave to swaying. Together. The static that is in us all at varying degrees if we listen overwhelmed the television set. *Men and women.* The reporter's voice sputtered. *To remain separate at weddings.* All but the bubbles now. *Stained family's honor.*

Afternoon came to be after a pair of Bengali soldiers dressed in camouflage so bright eyes could hear it grated the iron gates against the concrete ground and loudly locked the latches at my approaching. This happened in nearly identical fashion three separate times in five minutes. The third time shook me up because the sounds of dragging gates and the hacking cough then spit from the guard felt five minutes familiar. Easier for the guards to let the harshness of metal against itself or concrete communicate than drill up energy and do it themselves. No matter. It's all music. The notes of which guided me to one dead end after another until I reached a dead end.

With a hut that looked so dark inside from the bright outside that all I saw at first were white eyes. It's June here in Bangladesh, the start of rainy season, the time of ripe jackfruit and malaria in the Chittagong Hill Tracts. A certain heat began to build within me not so much at the grinding gates or stern stares but at their meaning. *No.* And at my own tenuous stance on the shipbreaking industry. These heats melded with the sun's to create a thrumming that mimed the drumming of hammer at the now visible shipbreaking yard. So when a few dudes with ripped shirts plop their bare feet in oiled mud to come greet you with huge smiles of curiosity and pitchers of some liquid you can hear pouring before it's poured you walk in and you sit at the oldest wooden table you've ever seen and you know everything is going to be okay though you know not who the hell you are with or where the hell you are.

Though Dhaka's 400,000 cycle rickshaws bestowed the "Rickshaw Capital of the World" title upon it, Chittagong is no slouch. If baritone horn played the soundtrack to the posture of the soldiers denying me, then inflating cycle rickshaw tire was the sound of my eased tension. Ten or more men of varying ages sat watching me from all angles. The elder of the bunch looked at me and raised the pitcher and his bushy white eyebrows while dropping his face slightly down—a human gesture beyond language that asks. I did.

"Tea," a boy around ten said.

The sound of pouring tea made me see: though a visual in memory or imagined experience can be greater than reality, real sound always trumps sound imagined.

"Yes, thank you."

"Where you from?" the boy asked.

"U.S.A."

As I sipped the steam rose from my cup and I followed its trail up into their faces all smiling and even laughing at the smile on mine. Outside the hut are grown and muscled men who are but dots on the top of ships bigger than buildings. Inside the hut we are all smiling because they keep saying "Obama" and they keep saying "Obama" because they know it is a sound from my home and seem to like him and I am saying "Obama" because it spurs the comfort sound of creasing smiles and smiles need no translation and because it is pride and it is somehow simultaneously sound in this moment of place in Chittagong, Bangladesh, and in Altoona, Pennsylvania.

Outside the hut a man enters the poultry pen and a thousand feathers shed then rise with the flapping and panic. Inside the hut I am breaking fry bread apart and dunking it into tea as they showed me and they are laughing and patting me on the back and I am hearing Bengali and hearing what I hope and I gave to the swaying and am tapping my feet to the outside's million tiny clanks, to how those tiny clanks accrue over six months to reduce cargo ship to toxic sheet metal music that is not good and good. I hear them all in me when I hear nothing.

___/ 108

AUTHOR NOTE

"Description" in Greek. An ekphrastic poem is a vivid description of a scene or, more commonly, a work of art. Through the imaginative act of narrating and reflecting on the "action" of a painting or sculpture, the poet may amplify and expand its meaning.

In the series of ekphrastic poems titled, ___/ 108, each poem refers to one of the 108 photos that were taken by Pierre Torset to tell the story of shipbreaking in Chittagong. Visit the link below to view the photos:

pierretorset.com/stories/shipbreaking/shipbreakers/

2 / 108

Bulbous shadow lines

we see not   the calloused hands

the way our frames

dip towards each other   link

our toxic socks beyond checkered pasts

lungi   liberation   lives

are always   tied   though not

always
            obvious.

3 / 108

The white tuft of beard
demands respect in the village

no more. Now, tucks behind
shoulder, filters the particles

of war zones and childhoods
of ocean in sky not eye level

of what tale a camera captures
of how injury may be the best

way to ride parts and pieces
of things of nothings to gray.

6/108

Where there are ladders
there are climbers reaching

and where there are bottom
rungs there are dark dreams

deferred of crawling into holes
and being gone but for baby

anchored, hopefully, still, back
in Dhaka, whose fingers reach

rattle and shake it gently now
and harder later.

8/108

Dig deep, we're told.
Our bodies fold in half.
The old shrug, say us
young are too weak
when they see us itch
the tingle after numb.
This is how it happens.
How boys become men.
The old know well
the well of weakness.
They hand us theirs
to wear. An anchor
becomes a necklace.

9/108

"The great hero, being defeated in a face to face battle,
Beerbahu, leaves to the dead man's world,
at an earlier age…"

(সম্মুখ সমরে পড়ি, বীর-চূড়ামণি
বীরবাহু, চলি যবে গলা যমপুরে
অকালে…)

—Opening lines of Michael Madhusudan Dutta's
"The Saga of Meghnad's Killing" (1861)

10/208

You remember   coils
    when you see them.

The snake's tight ball of muscle.
    The butchered's bleeding out.

The yarn's tight ball of blessings.
    The cable's unrelenting

lesson: We all unravel
eventually   whether we want it

whether we began as silk or gravel
or the rust of the tired in between.

19/208

Rotten toenails
creep to calves
carry vein chains
and family burden
a drug to follow
the sun's glare
the spark's flare
when it guides
eyes to the sweet
smell of dry heat.

20/108

Hell's an easy leap,
a manmade frame,
but what of those
who bend thick steel,
spontaneous creativity,
those who look left
or those tired of left,
walking right with blur
as their trusted guide.

34/108

We know not our ways
of protecting only that
most times
protecting feels right.

Some of our hands
can tell others where
we've been and why
we're worth a listen.

What of being almost
blue shrouding black?

Some of our hands
can listen and never
question and then tell
others where to go.

43 / 108

A shark protects
its eyes when it bites.

A boxer protects
his chin when he strikes.

Blues to the blowtorch
worker, whose ungoggled

eyes see not created beauty
but night nightened again,

whose being might pride
our faceful of steel temper.

44/108

"I ask for a moment's indulgence to sit by thy side. The works that I have in hand I will finish afterwards.

Away from the sight of thy face my heart knows no rest nor respite, and my work becomes an endless toil in a shoreless sea of toil."

—Opening Lines of Rabindranath Tagore's
"A Moments Indulgence" (1910)

45/108

Even the shoulder knows
help of cloth and hand.

Bare flesh knows help
of cloth and genetics.

Open eyes know help
of shadow but eyes know
not the help of hiding.

49/108

"She has broken my shore, I build hers."

—Jasimuddin (1903-1976)
from the poem, "Pratidan"

52/108

"Some day you will know I visited this city
You'll see my footprints are lying
Before the door of your apartment
With sheer neglect."

—Excerpt from Shahabuddin Nagari's
"I Came At Your Door"
The Black Cat and Other Poems (AuthorHouse, 2011)

55/108

"My wife has hanged herself
She could no longer bear hunger,
Now I plough deep into soil
In the hope of seeing her again."

—Jasimuddin,
"O Father Come Let Us Plough"

57/108

His white space rubbled smoke.
His own hair.
His own eyebrows.
His own smoke.
He owns some things in this world
and that's enough for him.
All jobs shape bodies—
writers carpal tunneled,
surgeons rotator cuffed,
little angels floating around
own seconds of naked breath.

65 / 108

Some look like they've been
around, as though they are
culling stories from corners
of the world as you speak,
as though. Some look like.
Some look like as though.

70/108

"In the dawn of life I see the sky, what I realise
Drops of sorrows are not in the eyes
hence I observe the scarlet hope of sun rise."

—Dilwar Khan,
a quote from the poet
in the profile, "A People's Poet"
The Daily Star (Vol. 8, Iss. 76)

73/108

"I'll take up from the damaged youthfulness
A container full of yearning for you.
Your white pairs of feet will be smeared with *Alta*
And will engage in the game of fire."

—Excerpt from Shahabuddin Nagari's
"A Container of Yearning"
The Black Cat and Other Poems (AuthorHouse, 2011)

79 / 108

"The singer alone does not make a song, there has to be someone who hears
Only from the marriage of two forces does music arise in the world
Where there is no love, where listeners are dumb, there never can be song."

—Rabindranath Tagore,
"Broken Song"
Translation: William Radice

87/108

"you used to hide your face
why did you allow them, then, to laugh
into the black clamour of the bank of your tank?"

—Al Mahmud,
"Comes More Not"
Translation: Sayeed Abubakar

88/108

"The light of anarchy is in front
Come along, O you who want to bathe in the
     sea of light
We shall board the ship of darkness tonight,
     Comrade,
Hold fast your hammer, pick up your shovel,
Sing in unison and advance."

—Kazi Nazrul Islam,
"Song of the Worker"
Translation: Kabir Chowdhury

91/108

"It's not mere turning off
but keeping the genius of eyes closed
from the attack of sight bent on the ground."

—Al Mahmud,
"Bent on the Ground"
Translation: Sayeed Abubakar

94/108

"Rising with a sudden start I see: my heart's monarch,
leaning in silence…"

—Sufia Kamal,
"Love-Timid"
Translation: Carolyne Wright, Ayesha Kabir

97/108

"A rose plant ceaselessly tells,
Plant me whether in the garden or cemetery…"

—Dilwar Khan,
a quote from the poet
in the profile, "A People's Poet"
The Daily Star (Vol. 8, Iss. 76)

99/108

"They ruled the world
while lived like a destitute;
Loss of a battle did not ruin their spirit,
this was their attitude."

—Kazi Nazrul Islam,
"Be Ever Stronger!"
Translation: Mohammad Omar Farooq

101/108

"I've taken possession of that love of yours
that fills the earth's vessel till it overflows,
filling my eyes, filling my heart,
          and filling my two hands."

—Sufia Kamal,
"That Love of Yours"
Translation: Carolyne Wright, Ayesha Kabir

101/108

No history here
but of what eyes caught
and mind tried
to make sense of.

101/108

But what of what eyes
caught and mind tried
to make sense of?

Acknowledgments

"Of Ships and Men," *Poetry for Freedom Anthology*, mid-2013

"Things Break Apart," *Spoke Journal*, December 2012

Special thanks to YPSA.org, FIDH.org and this report:

http://www.shipbreakingbd.info/report/Report_Childbreaking_Yards_2008.pdf

Works Cited

Page 13 • The opening Muhammad Yunus quote is from this source: http://knowledge.wharton.upenn.edu/article/muhammad-yunus-banker-to-the-worlds-poorest-citizens-makes-his-case/

Page 51 • Opening lines of Michael Madhusudan Dutta's poem. Here is the source: http://en.wikipedia.org/wiki/Meghnad_Badh_Kavya

Page 57 • A quote from a poem. Here is the source: http://rabindranathtagoreib.weebly.com/a-moments-indulgence.html

Page 59 • A quote from a poem. Here is the source: http://en.wikipedia.org/wiki/Jasimuddin

Page 60 • A quote from a poem. Here is the source: http://www.amazon.com/dp/1463413696/ref=rdr_ext_tmb

Page 61 • A quote from a poem. Here is the source: http://sos-arsenic.net/lovingbengal/jasi-poems.html

Page 64 • A quote from a profile about the poet. Here is the source: http://archive.thedailystar.net/magazine/2009/07/01/profile.htm

Page 65 • A quote from a poem. Here is the source. NOTE: It is the same source as Page 60: http://www.amazon.com/dp/1463413696/ref=rdr_ext_tmb

Page 66 • A quote from a poem. Here is the source: http://www.jstor.org/discover/10.2307/3517549?uid=3739864&uid=2129&uid=2&uid=70&uid=4&uid=3739256&sid=21104132759181

Page 67 • A quote from a poem. Here is the source: http://www.poemhunter.com/i/ebooks/pdf/al_mahmud_2012_3.pdf

Page 68 • A quote from a poem. Here is the source: http://www.nazrul.org/nazrul_works/poems_lyrics/kabir_worker.htm

Page 69 • A quote from a poem. Here is the source: http://www.poemhunter.com/poem/bent-on-the-ground/

Page 70 • A quote from a poem. Here is the source: http://foundationsaarcwriters.com/Padma%20meghna%20jamuna.pdf

Page 71 • A quote. Here is the source. (same source as Page 64): http://archive.thedailystar.net/magazine/2009/07/01/profile.htm

Page 72 • A quote from a poem. Here is the source. http://www.nazrul.org/nazrul_works/farooq_trans/t_naz_stronger.htm

Page 73 • A quote from a poem. Here is the source: (same source as Page 70) http://foundationsaarcwriters.com/Padma%20meghna%20jamuna.pdf

Cameron Conaway is a former MMA fighter, an award-winning poet and the 2014 Emerging Writer-in-Residence at Penn State Altoona. While serving as the Poet-in-Residence at the Mahidol Oxford Tropical Medicine Research Unit in Thailand, Conaway wrote *Malaria, Poems* (Michigan State University Press, 2014), the first full-length book of contemporary poetry about malaria's impact on the world. He served as a 2014 Social Good Fellow through the United Nations Foundation and as a Rotary International End Polio Now "HistoryMaker." Conaway is the author of *Caged: Memoirs of a Cage-Fighting Poet* (Threed Press, 2011), *Bonemeal* (Finishing Line Press, 2014) and *Until You Make the Shore* (Salmon Poetry, 2014). He is on the editorial board at *Slavery Today: A Multidisciplinary Journal of Human Trafficking Solutions*. Follow him on Twitter @CameronConaway.

CPSIA information can be obtained at www.ICGtesting.com
Printed in the USA
LVOW08s1438290316

481257LV00005B/582/P

9 781604 542257